The Gardener's

Color Guide

Designing the Flower Garden by Color and Season

Edited by Jane Good · Illustrated by Turid Forsyth

Canadian Cataloguing in Publication Data

Good, Jane, 1948-
   The gardener's color guide

ISBN 0-921820-67-4

1. Color in gardening.   I. Title.

SB454.3.C6+C66 1993   635.9'68   C93-093438-5

Published by Camden House Publishing
(a division of Telemedia Communications Inc.)

Camden House Publishing
7 Queen Victoria Road
Camden East, Ontario K0K 1J0
Canada M2H 2S4

Camden House Publishing
Box 766
Buffalo, New York 14240-0766

Trade distribution by
Firefly Books
250 Sparks Avenue
Willowdale, Ontario
Canada M2H 2S4

Box 1325
Ellicott Station
Buffalo, New York 14205

Design by
Linda J. Menyes

Photographs by
Turid Forsyth

Colour separations by
Chroma Graphics Pte. Ltd.
Singapore

Printed and bound in Canada by
D.W. Friesen & Sons Ltd.
Altona, Manitoba

Printed on acid-free paper

Acknowledgements

Like a healthy garden, this book has benefited from being well tended by many encouraging hands throughout its seasons of growth. Thanks to horticulturist Lawrence Sherk for verifying the selection and hardiness of the plants; to advisors Ulrike Bender, Patricia Denard-Hinch, Cheryl Jelley, Janice McAvoy, Marg Phelan, Lois Robertson, Lois Smith and Virginia Thompson for sharing their gardens and their gardening knowledge; to the Camden House team of art director Linda Menyes, editor Tracy Read, assistant editor Mary Patton, editorial production consultant Susan Dickinson and associates Catherine DeLury and Christine Kulyk for cultivating the project; and especially to Turid Forsyth, gardener, photographer and illustrator, for capturing the colors of the garden on the printed page.

—*Jane Good, Editor*

Contents

Introduction

"To plant and maintain a flower border with a good scheme for color is by no means the easy thing that it is commonly supposed." Despite these words of caution, Gertrude Jekyll, renowned garden designer and garden writer, understood the profound pleasures and the glimpses of glory that tempt us to try. Every garden—real or imagined, in a painting, a photograph or just outside the door—is a palette of promise. Offering advice and encouragement, Jekyll continues: "To devise these living pictures from simple, well-known flowers seems to me to be the best thing to do in gardening." We heartily agree.

Bringing about and maintaining good color in the garden can be challenging, rewarding and, just as important, fun. Yet coming to recognize the value of color can sometimes take a while. For many seasons—and for many good reasons—it is possible to be completely unaware of a garden's rich tapestry, as we take for granted the many hues and tones that nature paints. But at some moment, that changes. Garden color takes on new meaning. Whether we are happy simply to enjoy the gardens that others create or keen to dig in and weave our own botanical cloth, we greet this new awareness with anticipation and pleasure.

Fortunately, good use of color has as much to do with personal preferences as with principles and rules. By trying different groupings and by moving plants from place to place, gardeners often develop fine color combinations naturally, without knowing any rules. Whether you have little or lifelong experience, you come to know what you like when you see it, and when you see something displeasing, you try to avoid it. But sometimes, when the process of learning seems limited to trial and error and procrastination is a too familiar alternative, you crave a little help. We hope you will find that help—and insight and inspiration—here.

One simple way of working with colors is to arrange them in complementary pairs. For each primary color (red, yellow, blue), there is, conveniently enough, a corresponding complementary color (green, purple, orange). The partners enhance each other by providing contrast in brightness, intensity and warmth. The greatest contrast in brightness is with the yellow-purple pair. Spring-flowering lemon day lilies will therefore emphasize the clarity of color in deep purple irises.

Something else to take into account is the balance of intensities or, in other words, the richness or paleness of colors. While the contrast of blue and orange—a complementary pair—can be beautiful, the delicate blue of pincushion flower might look washed out against the rich orange of Cali-

fornia poppies. It might be more satisfying to plant pincushion flower with a pastel peach lychnis and place the bright poppies beside the saturated sky-blue of perennial flax.

Through experience, you will become sensitive to the play between warm and cool colors. Generally, yellow, orange and red are referred to as warm colors, while blue and purple are considered cool. However, to be more accurate, it is the amount of yellow in any color that determines its warmth and the proportion of blue that defines its coolness. Red, for example, can often straddle the warm-cool boundary. A red with a significant amount of yellow will lean toward orange and can be treated as a warm color, while a red with a touch of blue will appear more purple and fall in the cool range. Generally, you can achieve a pleasing effect by planting warm colors beside complementary cool colors. It can be a little trickier to blend several warm colors without clashing or many cool colors without losing vibrancy. Also, visual harmony is often easiest to create if you take care to establish a dominant color range and a lesser, supporting one, so that the two do not compete with each other for attention.

Known for her creative vision, Vita Sackville-West avoided both jarring and boring color combinations when she designed the all-white garden at Sissinghurst. A planting of many different whites —silvers, snow-whites, creams and greys—it is perhaps one of the most beautiful gardens in the world. As Sackville-West understood, white can stand alone and it can also be the key to the most

effective use of other colors. Although not a member of a complementary pair, it has the best capacity to reflect light, lending brightness to shade and counterpoint to color.

Of all the colors, the one that lures us most seductively to the garden is green. At first, it is new-growth green, that fresh, innocent, just-leafed-out spring green. Then, through the seasons, we watch it change, fascinated by the many greens of later growth. Greens lend a sense of continuity and rhythm to the garden, weaving together opposing colors and echoing the hues of the flowers around them. Often, a close look at the stem and foliage of a plant gives a welcome clue to its best position in the garden. Artemisia is as much grey as green; begonia foliage has a touch of red; and the leaves of garden phlox are tinged with purple. By using the nuances of green—and coincidentally adding variety in texture, form and height—you can alleviate the monotony of a monochromatic scheme or achieve harmony in a garden of many colors.

Just as in decorating or fashion, different colors in the garden can alter mood and perspective. Intense colors are bold, assertive and resonant, subdued colors are tranquil, serene and soothing. While vivid colors command attention and seem to move forward in our field of view, pastels and cool colors appear to recede. If your aim is to make a small yard look deeper, you could set out a foreground of brilliant, warm colors that blend into a planting of cooler, paler tones behind. If you want to enjoy all the detail of pastel flowers that might otherwise disappear in the distance, simply reverse the planting, placing pastels close by and setting plants with more vibrant color farther away.

When you are deciding on color combinations, keep in mind that the way you perceive color depends not only on the actual colors of the flowers and foliage but also on the quality of the light cast on them. Depending on many factors—the time of day, the season, the weather and the latitude—the kind of light your garden receives will change. In doing so, it also changes the way you perceive colors. The bright, direct light of midday, midsummer or hot-climate sun dilutes color, while the softer, indirect, more diffuse light of overcast skies, evening, early morning, springtime or temperate climates saturates it. Thus if you live in an area of bright summer sun and want your garden to be its most striking in midsummer or at midday, plant vivid, vibrant colors and avoid paler, softer shades, which will look weak and washed out.

If you will be viewing your garden under more diffuse light conditions, you will find that plantings of pastel colors, whites and grey-greens will come into their own. In this light, a large display of bright colors might be overwhelming and dark colors could be lost, although occasional brilliant accents can be very effective. The golden light of a low sun in late-day or late-season gardens is sympathetic to warm colors, while cool-color plantings benefit from the veiled light of early morning or springtime.

On the west side of his garden at Giverny, impressionist painter Claude Monet planted masses of rich orange, pink, gold and bronze flowers to capitalize on the effects of the setting sun. To give the illusion of soft, early-morning light in other areas of the garden, he planted clear blue and delicate salmon. Whether you are creating a beautiful painting or a garden, an understanding of the play of light can be of great advantage.

Where and how you plant color can be as important as the colors you plant. Drifts of color—slender swaths, set at an angle in the border, that overlap and intertwine—persuade the eye to follow them, rising here, sweeping there. Alternatively, punctuating the garden with accents of color encourages momentary pauses. Finally, taking into account the colors already in the garden—background plantings, additional structures and even the color of the house—is also important for achieving a harmonious effect.

In an attempt to simplify garden planning, we have grouped together plants that share the same season of prominent color. While we recognize that the onset, peak and demise of blooming vary according to weather patterns, geographic location,

available light and soil conditions, we assume that spring color continues into mid-June, summer reaches a peak in July and the transition to fall is in late August. Also, in the interest of being clear and accurate, we have included the botanical and well-known common names of each plant. When a particular hybrid or cultivar represents one aspect of a species' color range, its name appears in single quotation marks following the botanical name.

The color bands and sample-garden illustrations shown for each season feature annuals, biennials, perennials and bulbs that are, for the most part, quite well known, although we hope you will find some that are new to you. All have been chosen because of their value in providing extended, varied or continuous garden color and because they are readily available at reasonable cost, reliably hardy and adaptable to different regions and garden sites. Many have merit for additional reasons, such as scent, effectiveness as cut flowers and variation in texture and form of flowers or foliage. An added bonus is that most multiply readily or, in the case of annuals, self-seed easily, ensuring an ever-increasing supply of garden color and an ever-growing list of friends who will want a share in the bounty.

For each season, there is a series of color-band illustrations followed by an illustration of a sample garden. Useful for plant identification and for color planning, the color bands are set out in a progression of shades in various color ranges and feature plants that bloom at some time during the season. Attention has been paid to plant size,

growth habit and details of flowers and foliage. The sample gardens, different from one another in design and layout, suggest groupings of plants that mutually enhance one another either by contrast or by complement and include only those plants which contribute to maximum color at the midpoint of the season.

While the plant list is not exhaustive and the sample plantings are not intended to be prescriptive (very few of us want a garden that is colorful in only one season), we hope that they will make it easier for you to plan for overall color. The text accompanying each illustration and the charts on pages 32-34 include further information so that you can evaluate the appropriateness of the plants for your garden and consider alternatives. And to supplement the insights we hope you will gain from this book, we recommend reading any of the titles in the list on page 35, talking with friends and the staff at nearby nurseries about local sources for suggested or alternative cultivars and visiting other gardens for inspiration.

But as with most things, practice makes perfect. To get a sense of pleasing color combinations before committing yourself to a planting, try arranging cut flowers. And when a newcomer or a difficult-to-match plant is in bloom, place beside it cut blossoms or potted samples of potential companions, and stand back to assess the value of the proposed partnership. Above all, plant. With either whimsy or well-considered plans, plant. For the only thing that can match the pleasure of having a beautiful garden is the joy of creating it.

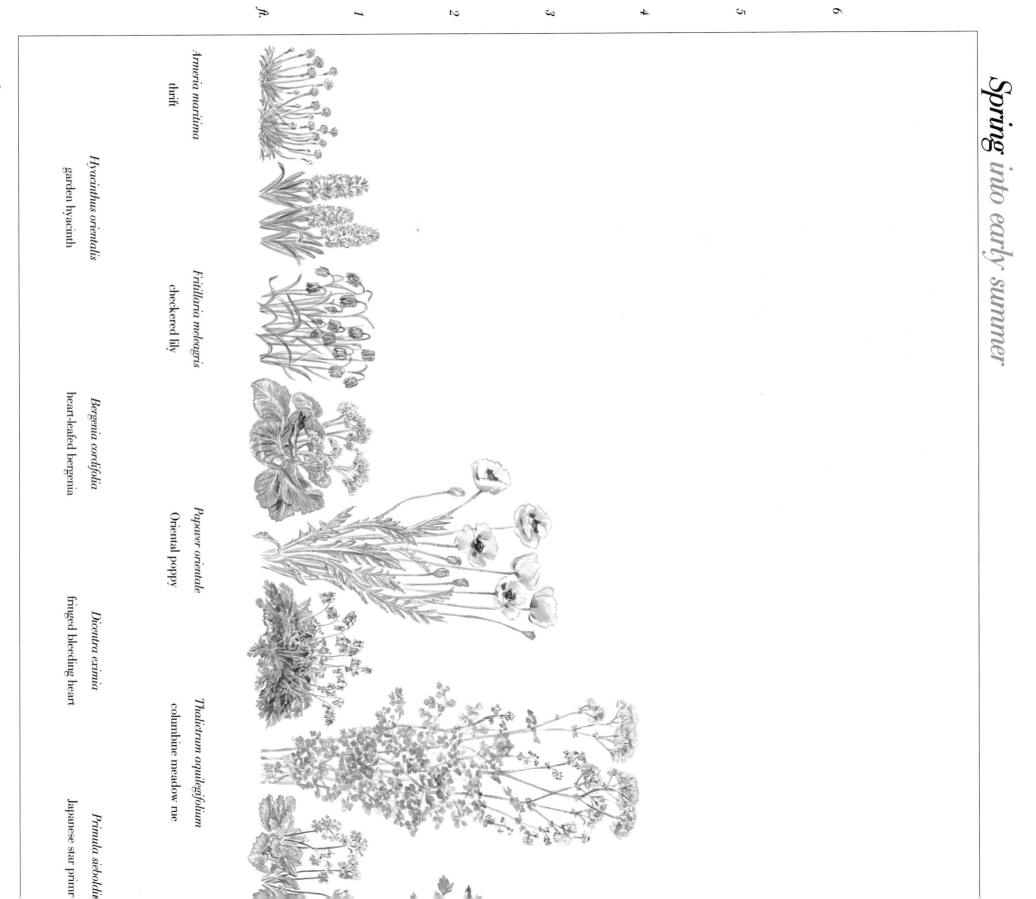

ft.
1
2
3
4
5
6

Armeria maritima
thrift

Hyacinthus orientalis
garden hyacinth

Fritillaria meleagris
checkered lily

Bergenia cordifolia
heart-leafed bergenia

Papaver orientale
Oriental poppy

Dicentra eximia
fringed bleeding heart

Thalictrum aquilegifolium
columbine meadow rue

Primula sieboldii
Japanese star primr

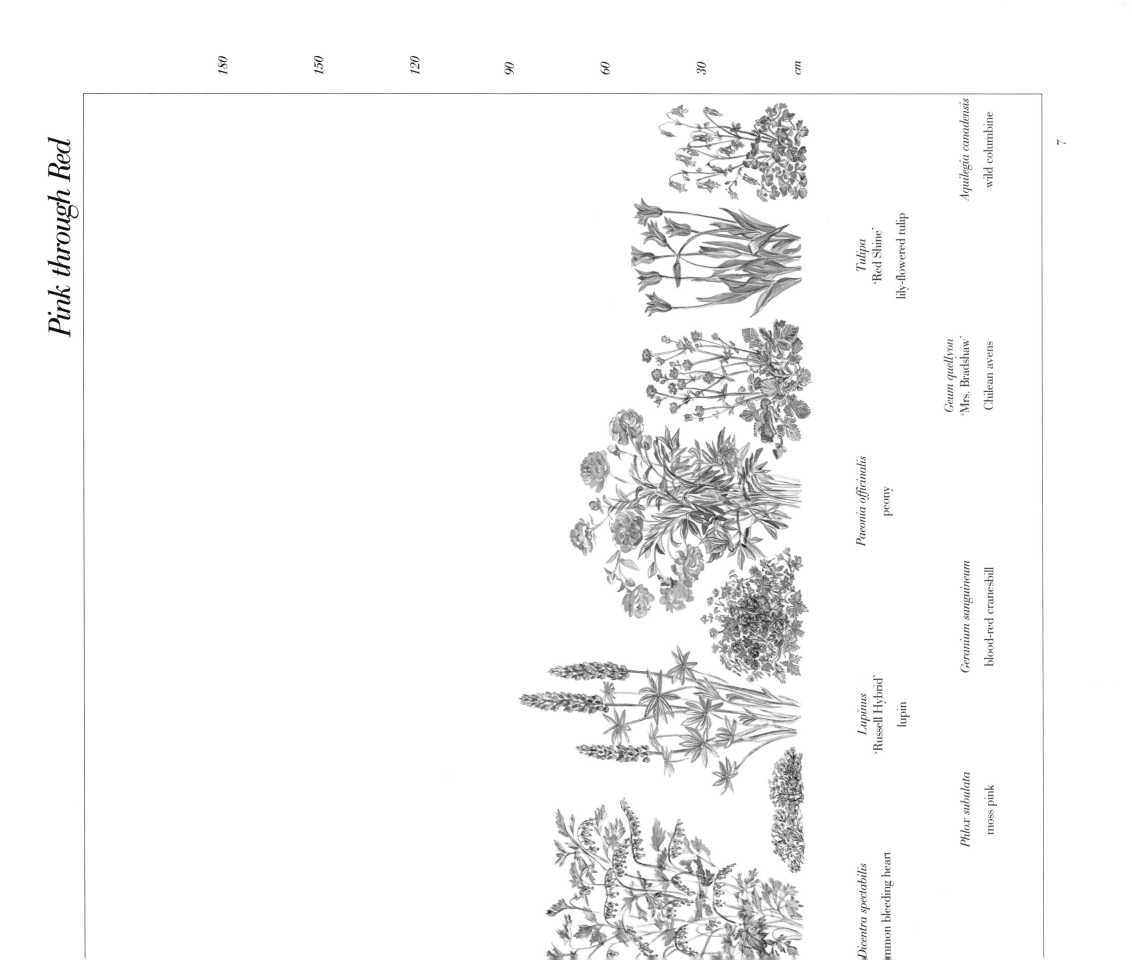

Pink through Red

180
150
120
90
60
30
cm

Aquilegia canadensis
wild columbine

Tulipa
'Red Shine'
lily-flowered tulip

Geum quellyon
'Mrs. Bradshaw'
Chilean avens

Paeonia officinalis
peony

Geranium sanguineum
blood-red cranesbill

Lupinus
'Russell Hybrid'
lupin

Phlox subulata
moss pink

Dicentra spectabilis
common bleeding heart

Crocus vernus
Dutch crocus

Aubrieta deltoidea
false rock cress

Viola tricolor
Johnny-jump-up

Aquilegia atrata
columbine

Anemone pulsatilla
pasqueflower

Iris sibirica
Siberian iris

Allium giganteum
giant onion

Muscari armeniacum
grape hyacinth

ft.

1

2

3

4

5

6

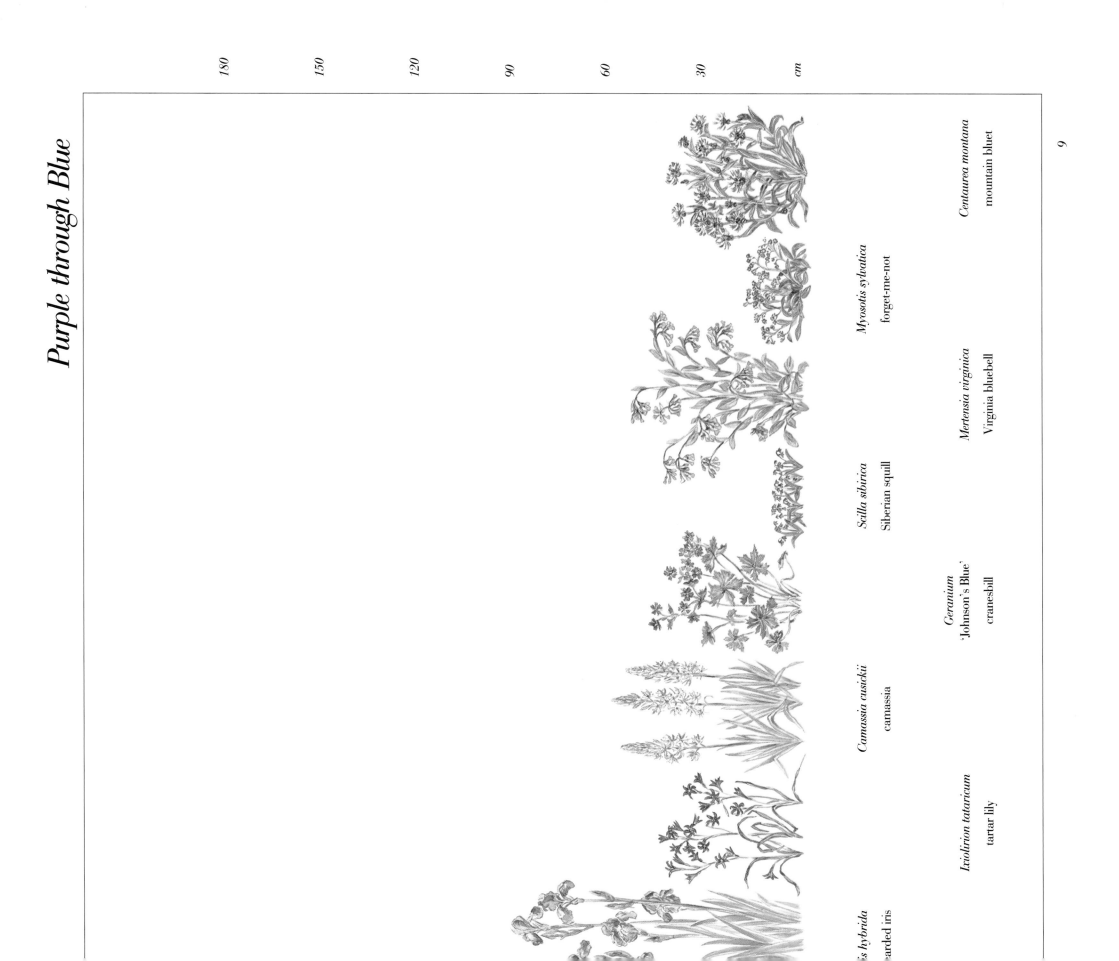

Purple through Blue

180

150

120

90

60

30

cm

Centaurea montana
mountain bluet

Myosotis sylvatica
forget-me-not

Mertensia virginica
Virginia bluebell

Scilla sibirica
Siberian squill

Geranium
'Johnson's Blue'
cranesbill

Camassia cusickii
camassia

Ixiolirion tataricum
tartar lily

s hybrida
earded iris

Anemone blanda
'White Splendour'
windflower

Puschkinia scilloides
striped squill

Tulipa
'Diana'
single-flowered tulip

Galanthus nivalis
common snowdrop

Paeonia officinalis
peony

Helleborus niger
Christmas rose

Polygonatum odoratum
Solomon's seal

Eremurus robus
foxtail lily

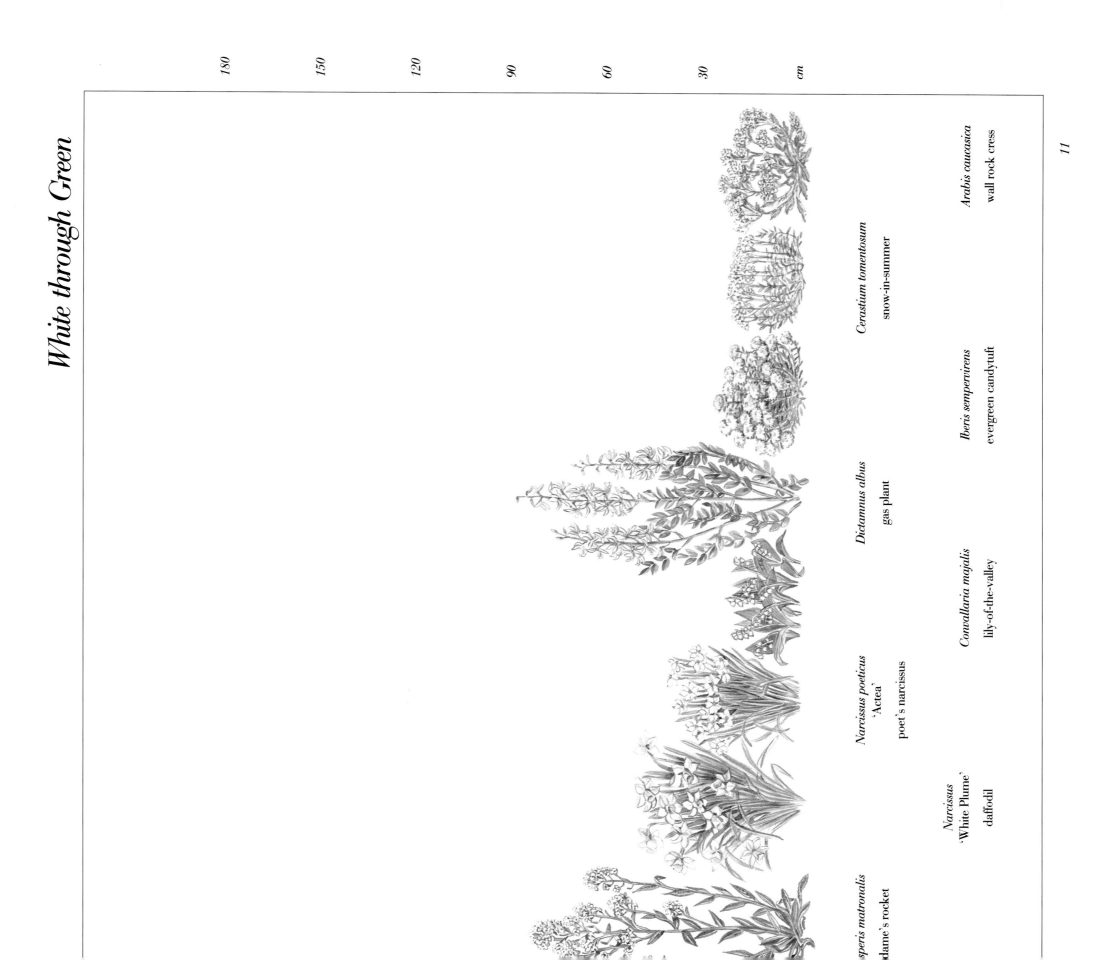

180

150

120

90

60

30

cm

Cerastium tomentosum
snow-in-summer

Arabis caucasica
wall rock cress

Dictamnus albus
gas plant

Iberis sempervirens
evergreen candytuft

Narcissus poeticus
'Actea'
poet's narcissus

Convallaria majalis
lily-of-the-valley

Narcissus
'White Plume'
daffodil

speris matronalis
dame's rocket

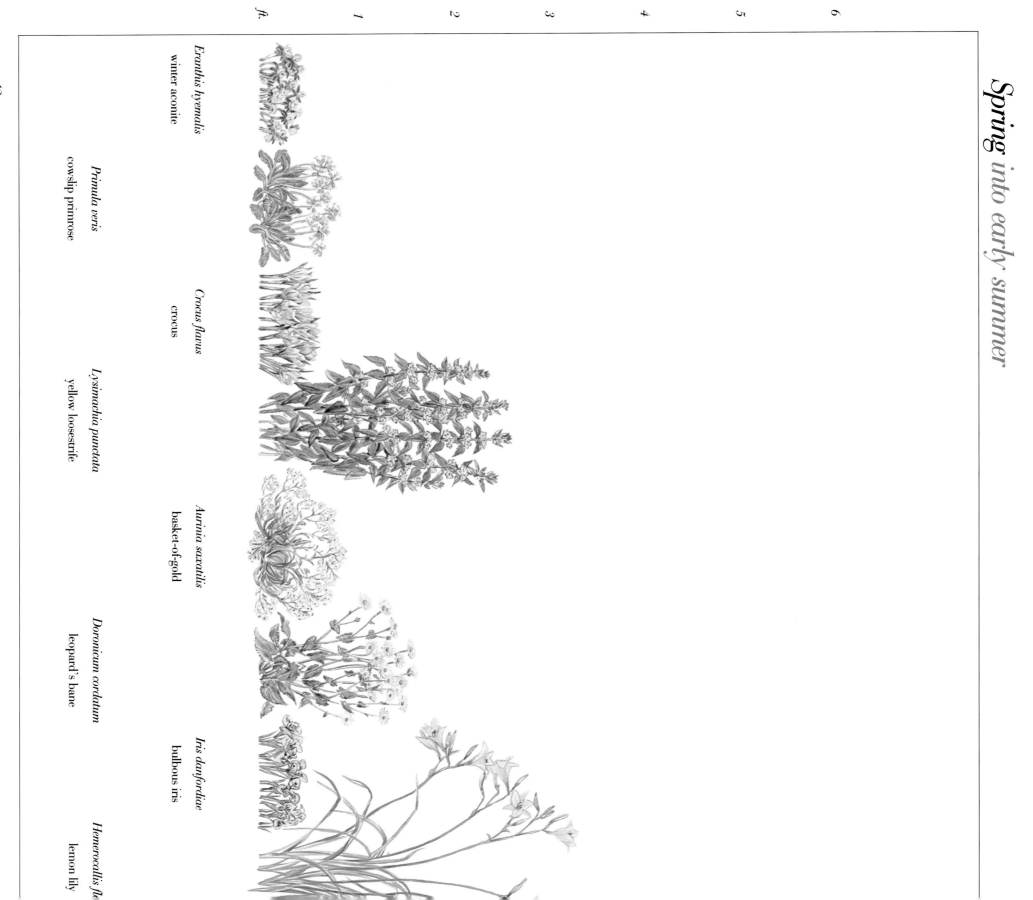

ft.

6

5

4

3

2

1

Eranthis hyemalis
winter aconite

Primula veris
cowslip primrose

Crocus flavus
crocus

Lysimachia punctata
yellow loosestrife

Aurinia saxatilis
basket-of-gold

Doronicum cordatum
leopard's bane

Iris danfordiae
bulbous iris

Hemerocallis fl...
lemon lily

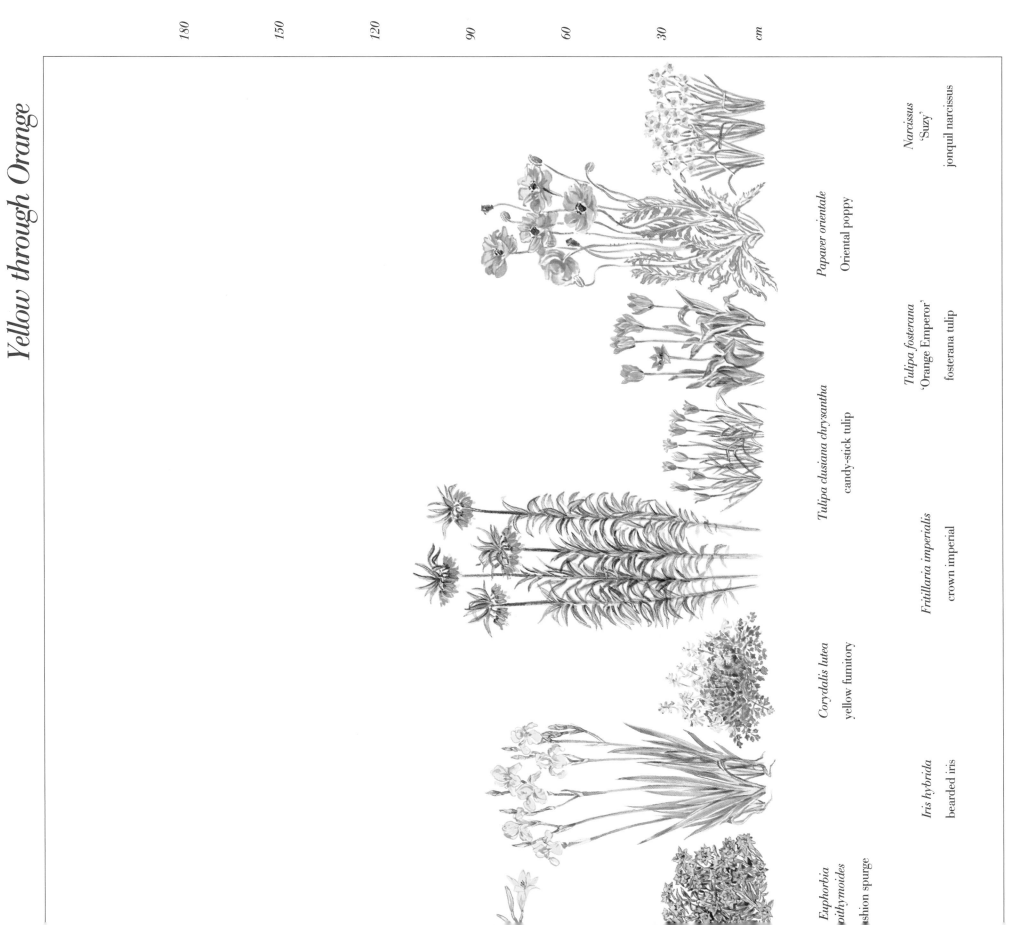

180

150

120

90

60

30

cm

Narcissus
'Suzy'
jonquil narcissus

Papaver orientale
Oriental poppy

Tulipa fosterana
'Orange Emperor'
fosterana tulip

Tulipa clusiana chrysantha
candy-stick tulip

Fritillaria imperialis
crown imperial

Corydalis lutea
yellow fumitory

Iris hybrida
bearded iris

*Euphorbia
epithymoides*
cushion spurge

With the same eagerness and determination of the first bulbs that flower, we were keen to take all that spring has to offer and blend it into this garden. To this end, we set pink and blue on the left and orange and red on the right. Then we joined the sides by weaving looping lines of repeated color—wisps of white, yarns of various yellows and a few tufts of deep purple—through the centre. In the left island, the drift of blue grape hya-

cinths, forget-me-nots and Virginia bluebells is fronted by pink hyacinths, bergenia and, just to the right of the white lily-of-the-valley, checkered lilies; the blues are backed by a group of red and white tulips and two forms of bleeding heart. Farther back is a repetition of the same colors: a flush of new peony growth, white Solomon's seal footed by grape hyacinths, budding blue irises and low-growing pink thrift. In the lightly shaded front left

corner, sunny yellow cowslip primroses beside the white aubrieta augment the fresh yellow-green of the foliage that appears throughout the island.

Beside the bleeding hearts, heading diagonally forward to the right, is a swath of white daffodils and tulips, snow-in-summer and, closer to the front, candytuft, sweeping toward the centre path, where the thread of blue continues as forget-me-nots weave into deep blue columbines and pur-

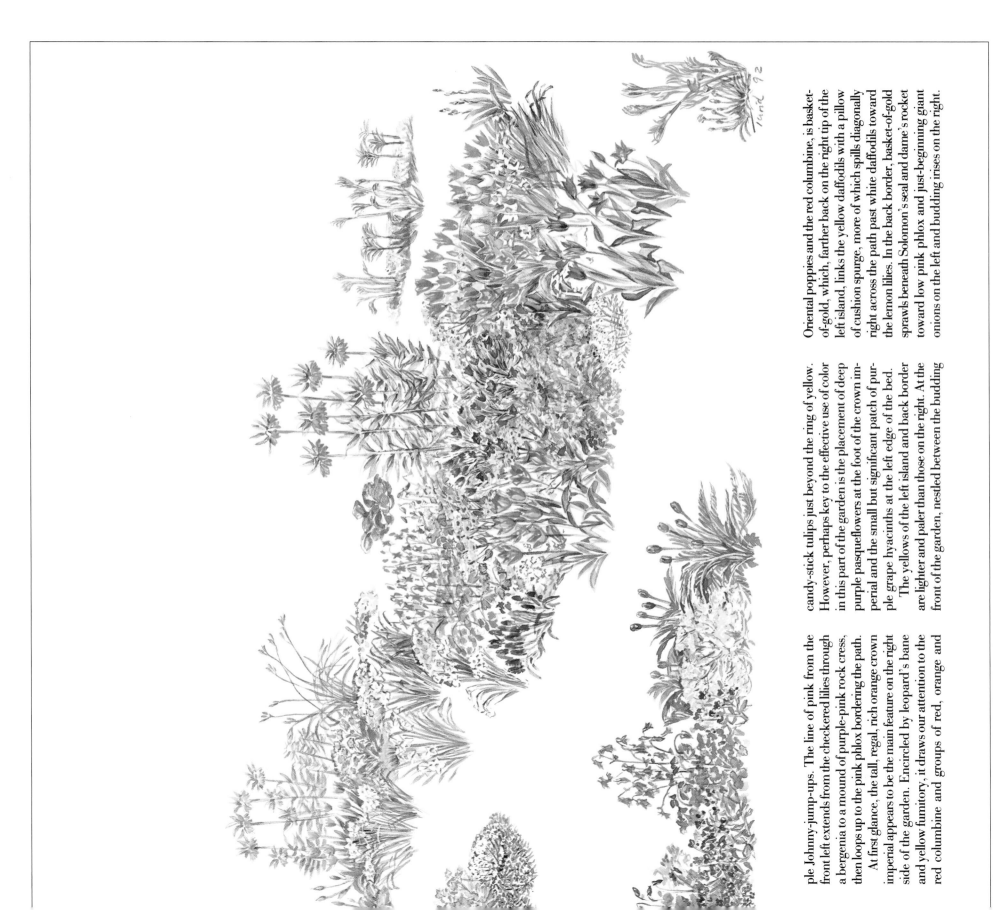

ple Johnny-jump-ups. The line of pink from the front left extends from the checkered lilies through a bergenia to a mound of purple-pink rock cress, then loops up to the pink phlox bordering the path.

At first glance, the tall, regal, rich orange crown imperial appears to be the main feature on the right side of the garden. Encircled by leopard's bane and yellow fumitory, it draws our attention to the red columbine and groups of red, orange and

candy-stick tulips just beyond the ring of yellow. However, perhaps key to the effective use of color in this part of the garden is the placement of deep purple pasqueflowers at the foot of the crown imperial and the small but significant patch of purple grape hyacinths at the left edge of the bed.

The yellows of the left island and back border are lighter and paler than those on the right. At the front of the garden, nestled between the budding

Oriental poppies and the red columbine, is basket-of-gold, which, farther back on the right tip of the left island, links the yellow daffodils with a pillow of cushion spurge, more of which spills diagonally right across the path past white daffodils toward the lemon lilies. In the back border, basket-of-gold sprawls beneath Solomon's seal and dame's rocket toward low pink phlox and just-beginning giant onions on the left and budding irises on the right.

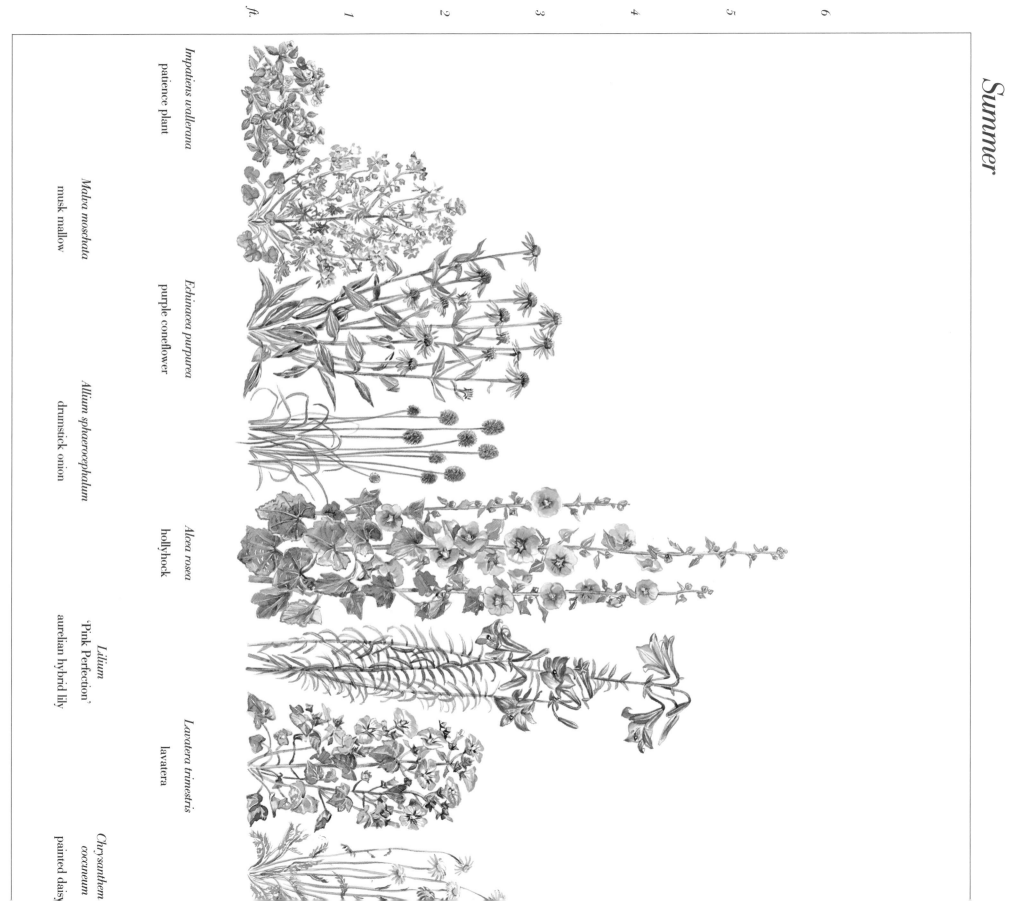

ft.
1
2
3
4
5
6

Impatiens wallerana
patience plant

Malva moschata
musk mallow

Echinacea purpurea
purple coneflower

Allium sphaerocephalum
drumstick onion

Alcea rosea
hollyhock

Lilium
'Pink Perfection'
aurelian hybrid lily

Lavatera trimestris
lavatera

Chrysanthem...
coccineum
painted dais...

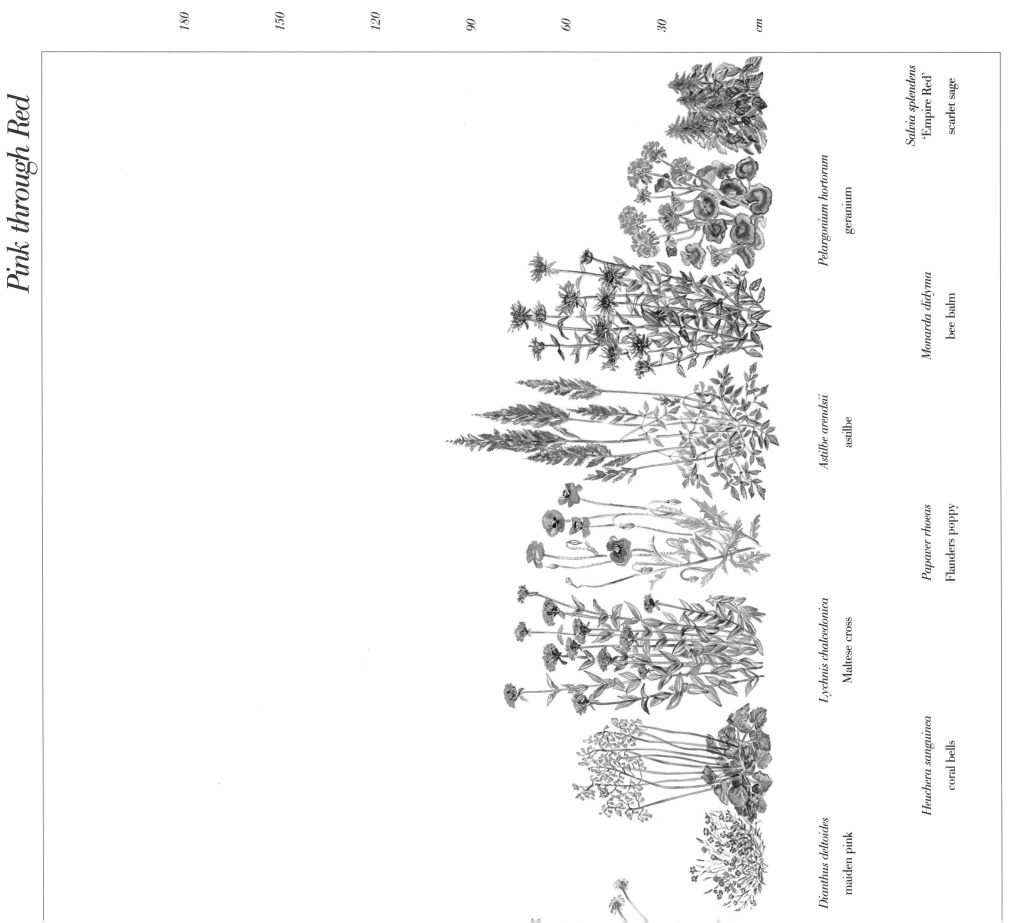

180

150

120

90

60

30

cm

Salvia splendens
'Empire Red'
scarlet sage

Pelargonium hortorum
geranium

Monarda didyma
bee balm

Astilbe arendsii
astilbe

Papaver rhoeas
Flanders poppy

Lychnis chalcedonica
Maltese cross

Heuchera sanguinea
coral bells

Dianthus deltoides
maiden pink

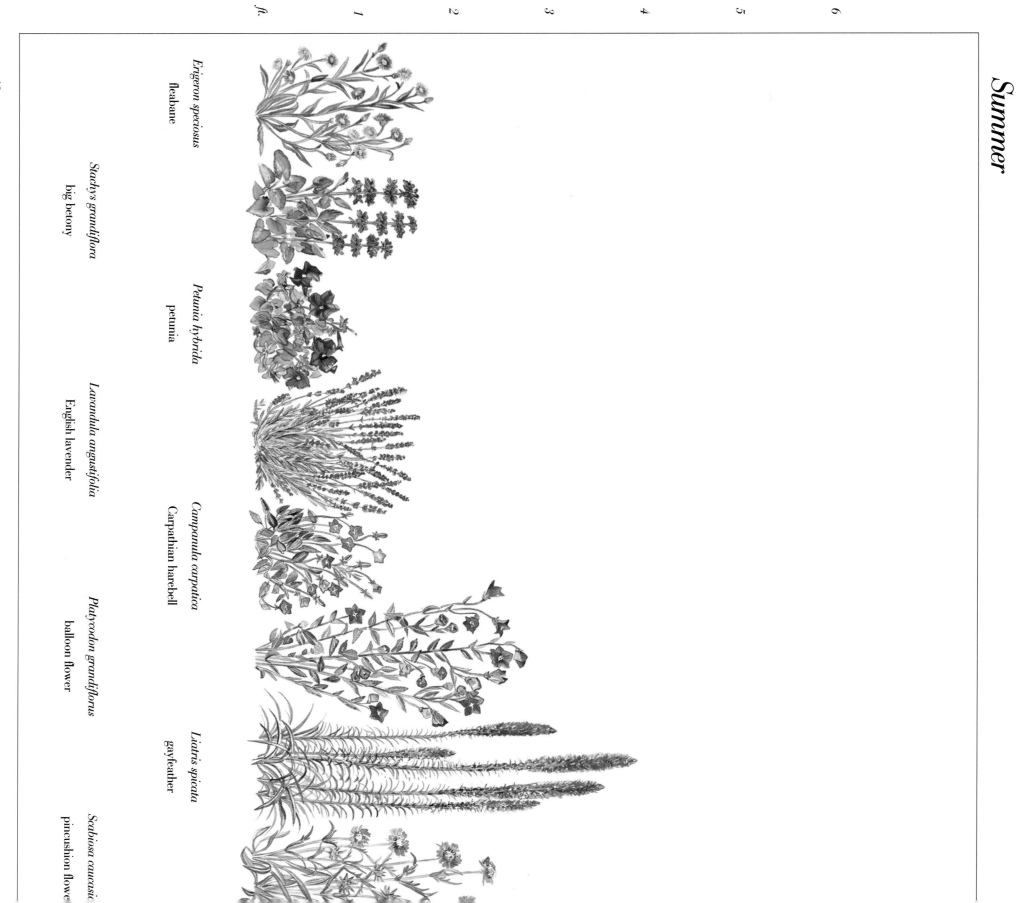

6

5

4

3

2

1

ft.

Erigeron speciosus
fleabane

Stachys grandiflora
big betony

Petunia hybrida
petunia

Lavandula angustifolia
English lavender

Campanula carpatica
Carpathian harebell

Platycodon grandiflorus
balloon flower

Liatris spicata
gayfeather

Scabiosa caucasica
pincushion flower

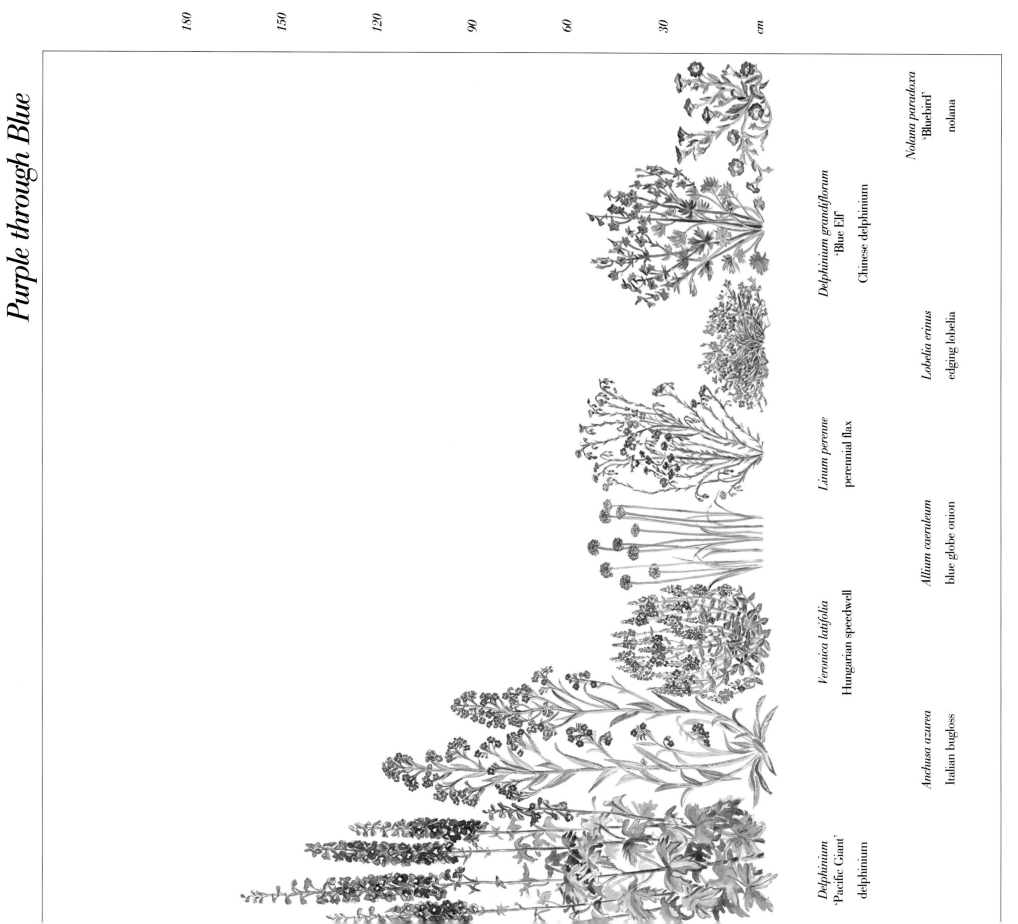

180

150

120

90

60

30

cm

Nolana paradoxa
'Bluebird'
nolana

Delphinium grandiflorum
'Blue Elf'
Chinese delphinium

Lobelia erinus
edging lobelia

Linum perenne
perennial flax

Allium caeruleum
blue globe onion

Veronica latifolia
Hungarian speedwell

Anchusa azurea
Italian bugloss

Delphinium
'Pacific Giant'
delphinium

Tradescantia andersoniana
spiderwort

Lobularia maritima
sweet alyssum

Antirrhinum majus
'Rockets'
snapdragon

Campanula persicifolia
peach-leafed bellflower

Iberis amara
giant hyacinth candytuft

Dianthus superbus
'Super Fantasy'
pink

Valeriana officinalis
valerian

Begonia tuberhybrid...
tuberous begonia

ft.

1

2

3

4

5

6

White through Green

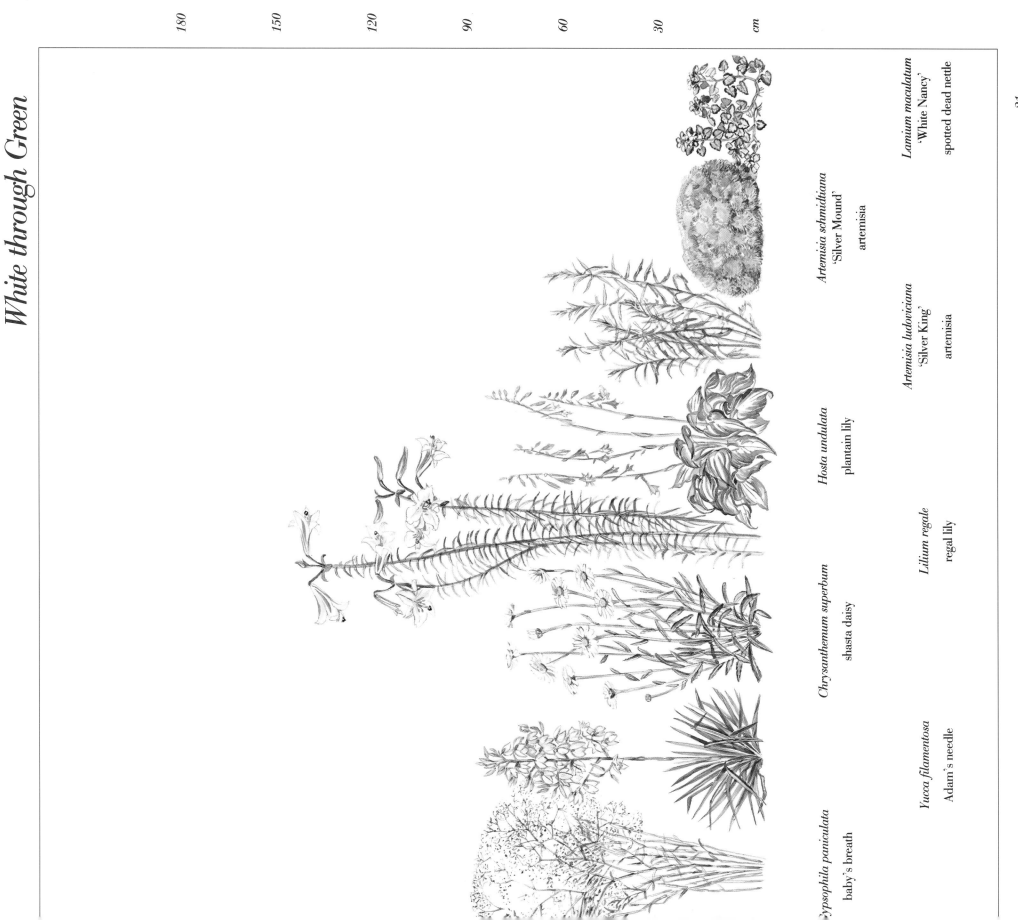

Scale (cm): 180, 150, 120, 90, 60, 30, cm

Lamium maculatum
'White Nancy'
spotted dead nettle

Artemisia schmidtiana
'Silver Mound'
artemisia

Artemisia ludoviciana
'Silver King'
artemisia

Hosta undulata
plantain lily

Lilium regale
regal lily

Chrysanthemum superbum
shasta daisy

Yucca filamentosa
Adam's needle

Gypsophila paniculata
baby's breath

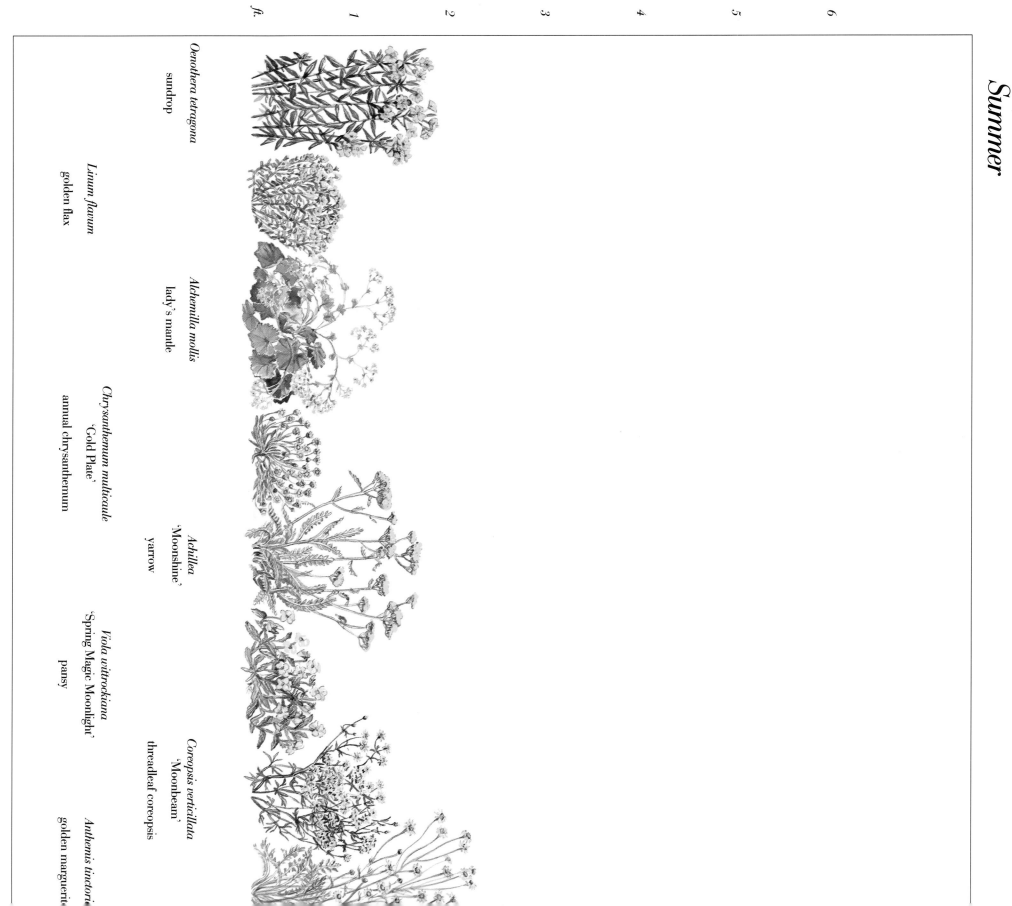

ft.

1

2

3

4

5

6

Oenothera tetragona
sundrop

Alchemilla mollis
lady's mantle

Linum flavum
golden flax

Achillea
'Moonshine'
yarrow

Chrysanthemum multicaule
'Gold Plate'
annual chrysanthemum

Coreopsis verticillata
'Moonbeam'
threadleaf coreopsis

Viola wittrockiana
'Spring Magic Moonlight'
pansy

Anthemis tinctoria
golden marguerite

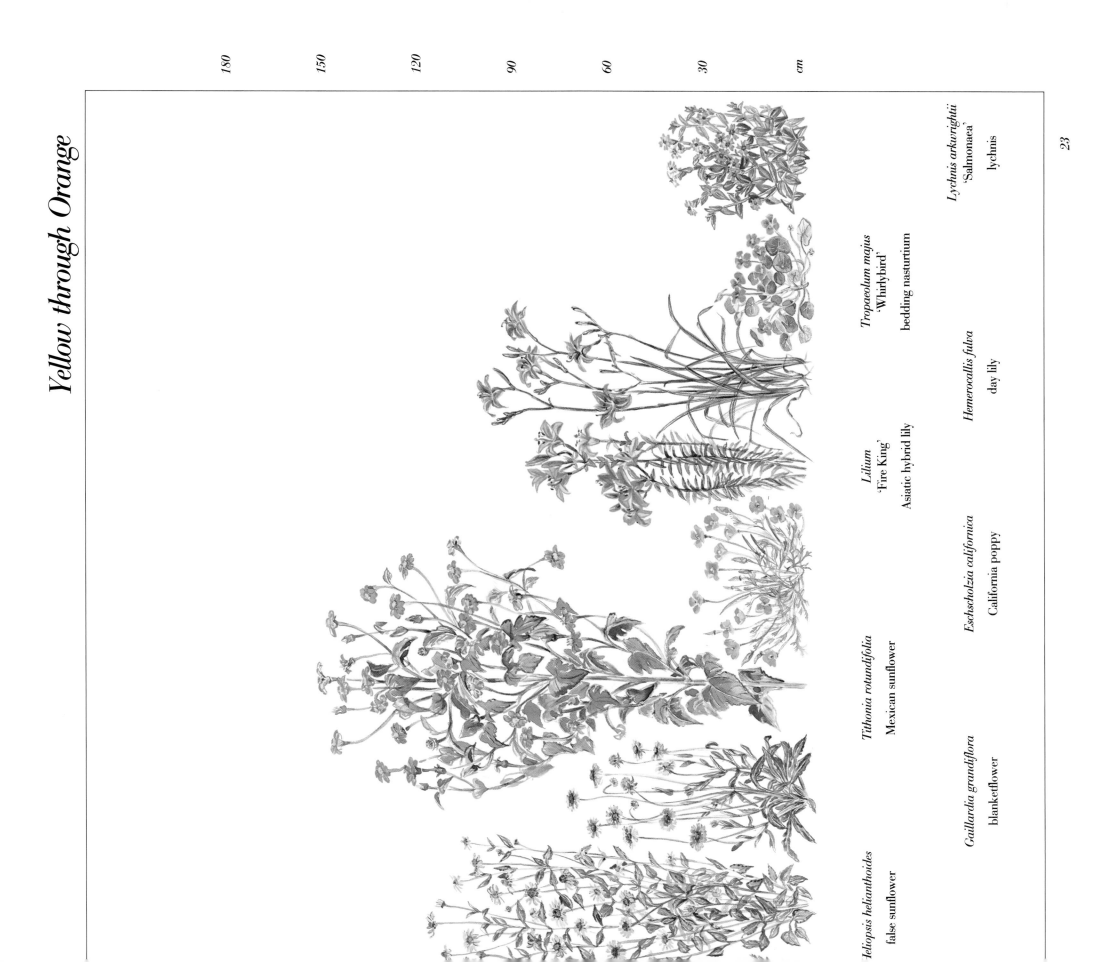

Yellow through Orange

180

150

120

90

60

30

cm

Lychnis arkwrightii
'Salmonaea'
lychnis

Tropaeolum majus
'Whirlybird'
bedding nasturtium

Hemerocallis fulva
day lily

Lilium
'Fire King'
Asiatic hybrid lily

Eschscholzia californica
California poppy

Tithonia rotundifolia
Mexican sunflower

Gaillardia grandiflora
blanketflower

Heliopsis helianthoides
false sunflower

Emerson's comment that the earth smiles in flowers might well have been prompted by a recollection of the gardens of summer—gardens filled with a welcoming array of color.

Given such diversity and the seemingly endless possibilities, we simplified planning by determining that we would select for particular single flower colors and avoid planting bicolors and mixes. Next, we decided to install specific groups of plants with effective color combinations, later weaving them into drifts with connecting plantings. Finally, we were aware that the left side of the garden receives full sun and that the only place we could locate shade-loving plants was in the front right. It was here that we started to plant.

We began with an impressive stand of deep blue giant delphiniums. They cast a little shade for the neighbouring hosta and the ground-hugging lamium. Crossing through the centre and back of

tiens and blue lobelia and maximize the illusion of coolness on a hot summer day. Significant, too, is the placement of the day lily. Arching stems topped by trumpets of orange complement the delphiniums and forge a link with the reaches of orange on the left side of the garden. Also, the verdant foliage contrasts in color and habit with the

red and pink astilbes, white begonias, pink impa-

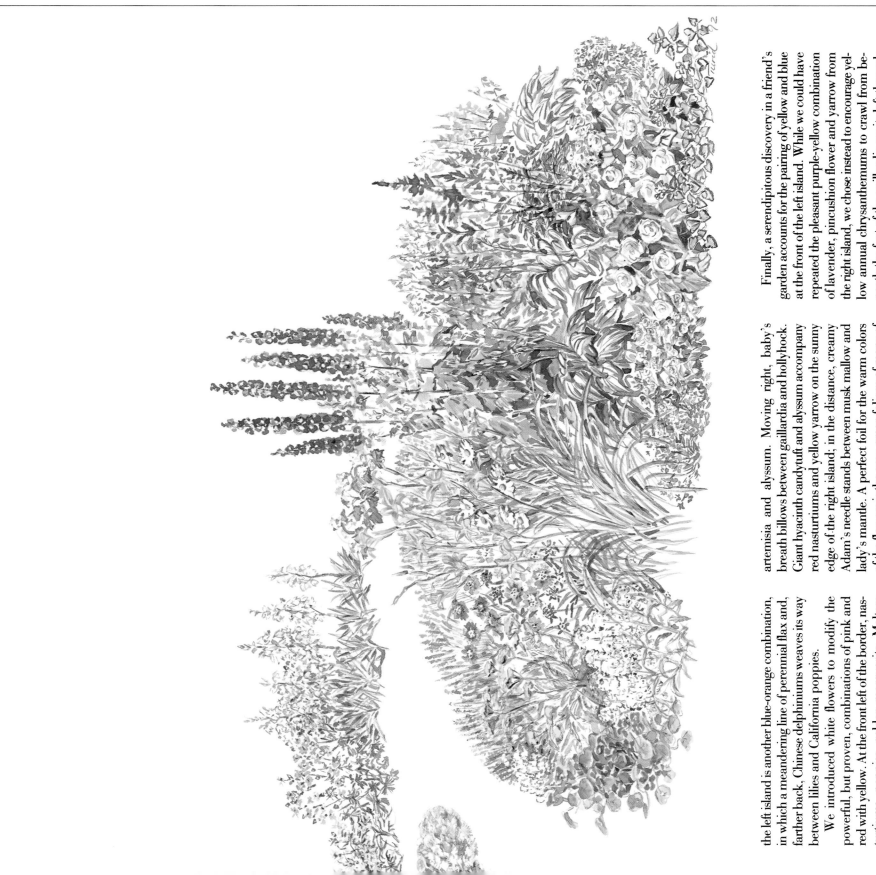

the left island is another blue-orange combination, in which a meandering line of perennial flax and, farther back, Chinese delphiniums weaves its way between lilies and California poppies.

We introduced white flowers to modify the powerful, but proven, combinations of pink and red with yellow. At the front left of the border, nasturtiums, poppies, golden marguerite, Maltese cross and purple coneflowers are planted behind

artemisia and alyssum. Moving right, baby's breath billows between gaillardia and hollyhock. Giant hyacinth candytuft and alyssum accompany red nasturtiums and yellow yarrow on the sunny edge of the right island; in the distance, creamy Adam's needle stands between musk mallow and lady's mantle. A perfect foil for the warm colors of the flowers is the grey-green foliage of many of these plants.

Finally, a serendipitous discovery in a friend's garden accounts for the pairing of yellow and blue at the front of the left island. While we could have repeated the pleasant purple-yellow combination of lavender, pincushion flower and yarrow from the right island, we chose instead to encourage yellow annual chrysanthemums to crawl from beneath the feet of the gaillardia on its left through a network of nolana into the yellow yarrow.

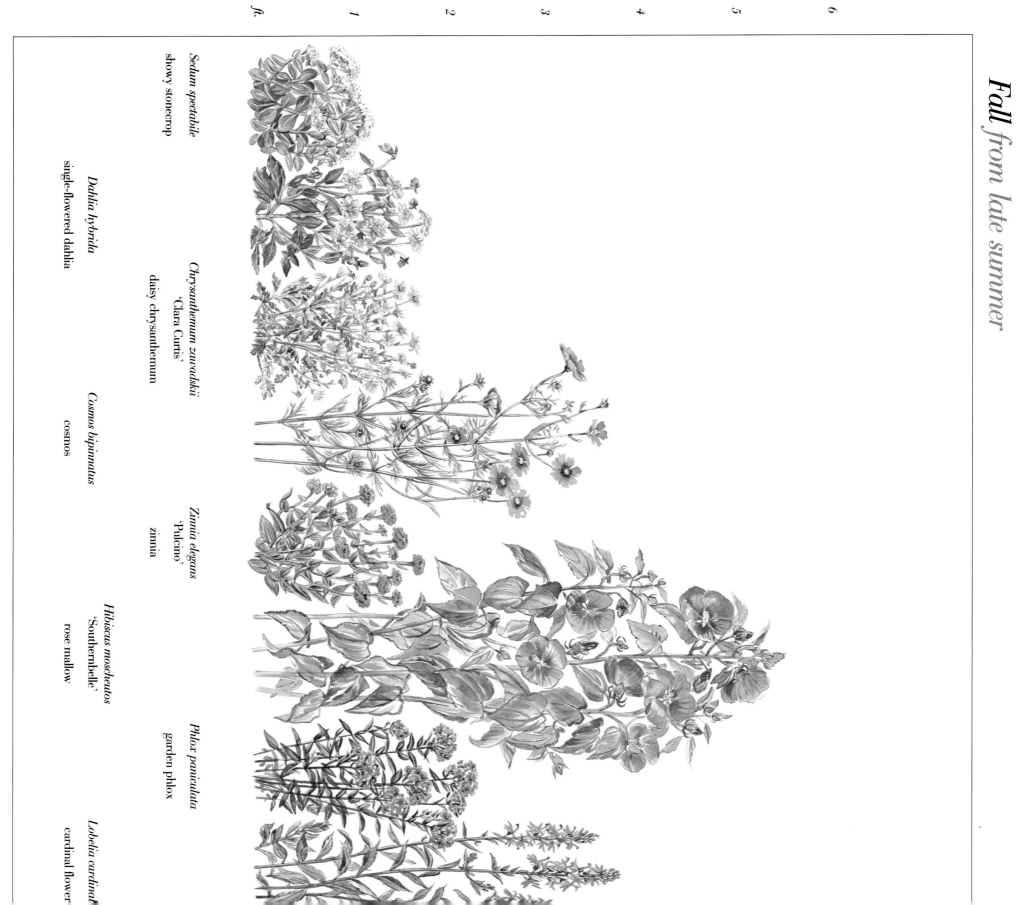

ft.

1

2

3

4

5

6

Sedum spectabile
showy stonecrop

Chrysanthemum zawadskii
'Clara Curtis'
daisy chrysanthemum

Dahlia hybrida
single-flowered dahlia

Cosmos bipinnatus
cosmos

Zinnia elegans
'Pulcino'
zinnia

Hibiscus moscheutos
'Southernbelle'
rose mallow

Phlox paniculata
garden phlox

Lobelia cardinal...
cardinal flower

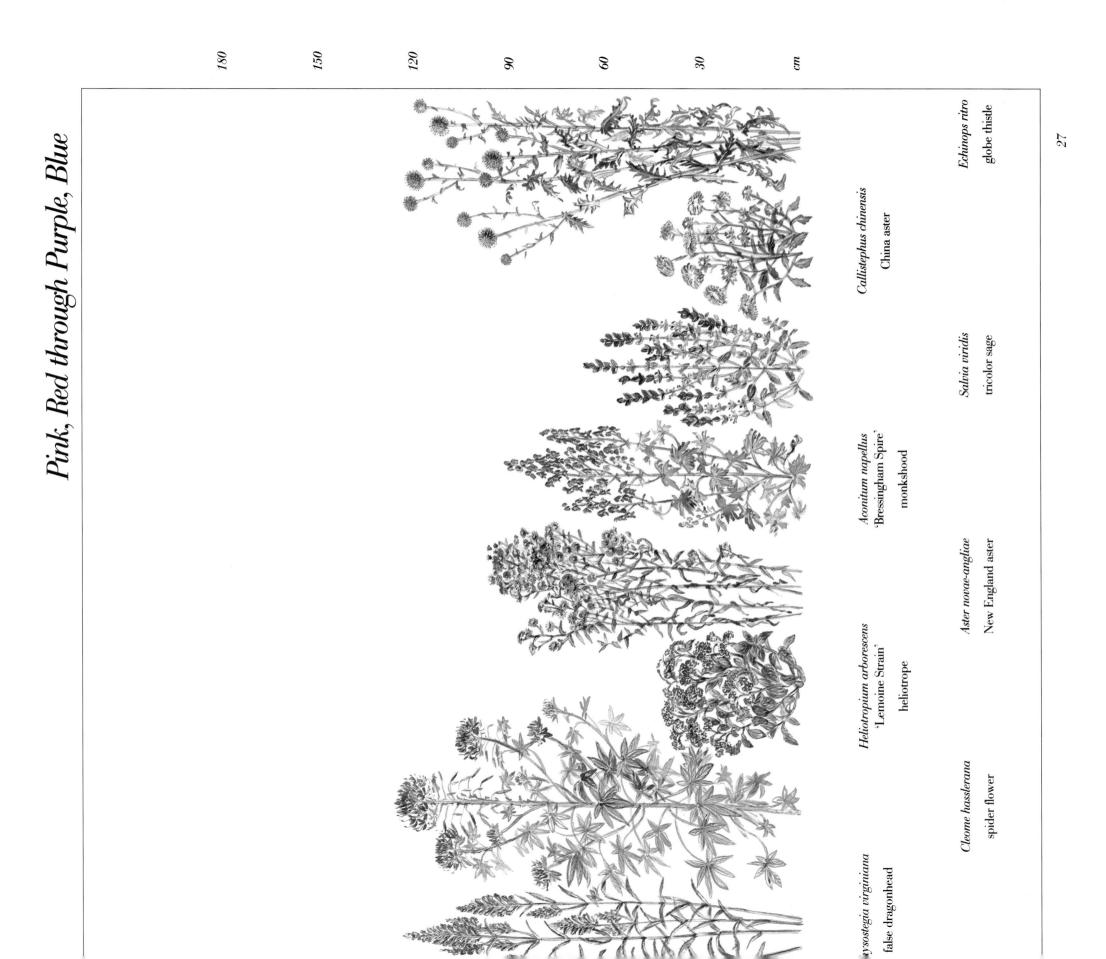

Pink, Red through Purple, Blue

180

150

120

90

60

30

cm

Echinops ritro
globe thistle

Callistephus chinensis
China aster

Salvia viridis
tricolor sage

Aconitum napellus
'Bressingham Spire'
monkshood

Aster novae-angliae
New England aster

Heliotropium arborescens
'Lemoine Strain'
heliotrope

Cleome hasslerana
spider flower

ysostegia virginiana
false dragonhead

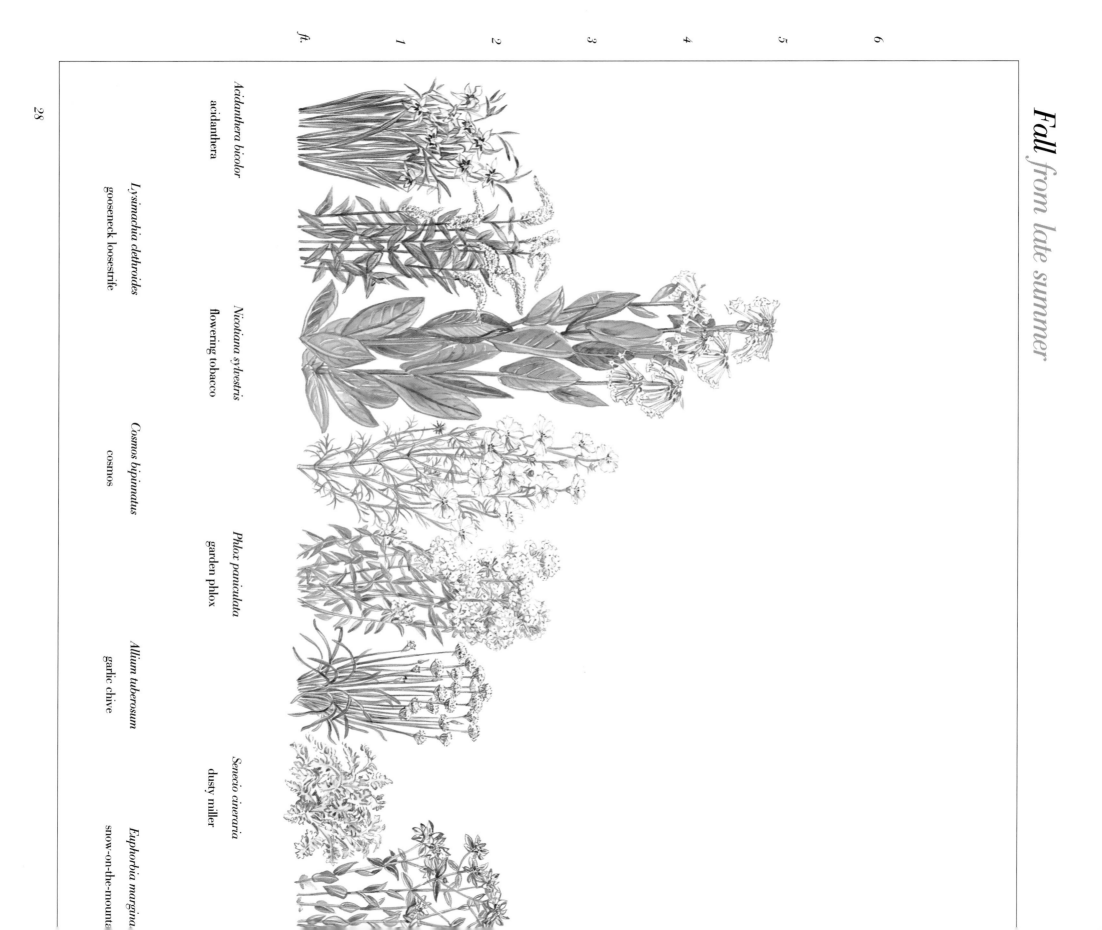

ft.

1

2

3

4

5

6

Acidanthera bicolor
acidanthera

Lysimachia clethroides
gooseneck loosestrife

Nicotiana sylvestris
flowering tobacco

Cosmos bipinnatus
cosmos

Phlox paniculata
garden phlox

Allium tuberosum
garlic chive

Senecio cineraria
dusty miller

Euphorbia marginata
snow-on-the-mountain

White, Green through Yellow, Orange

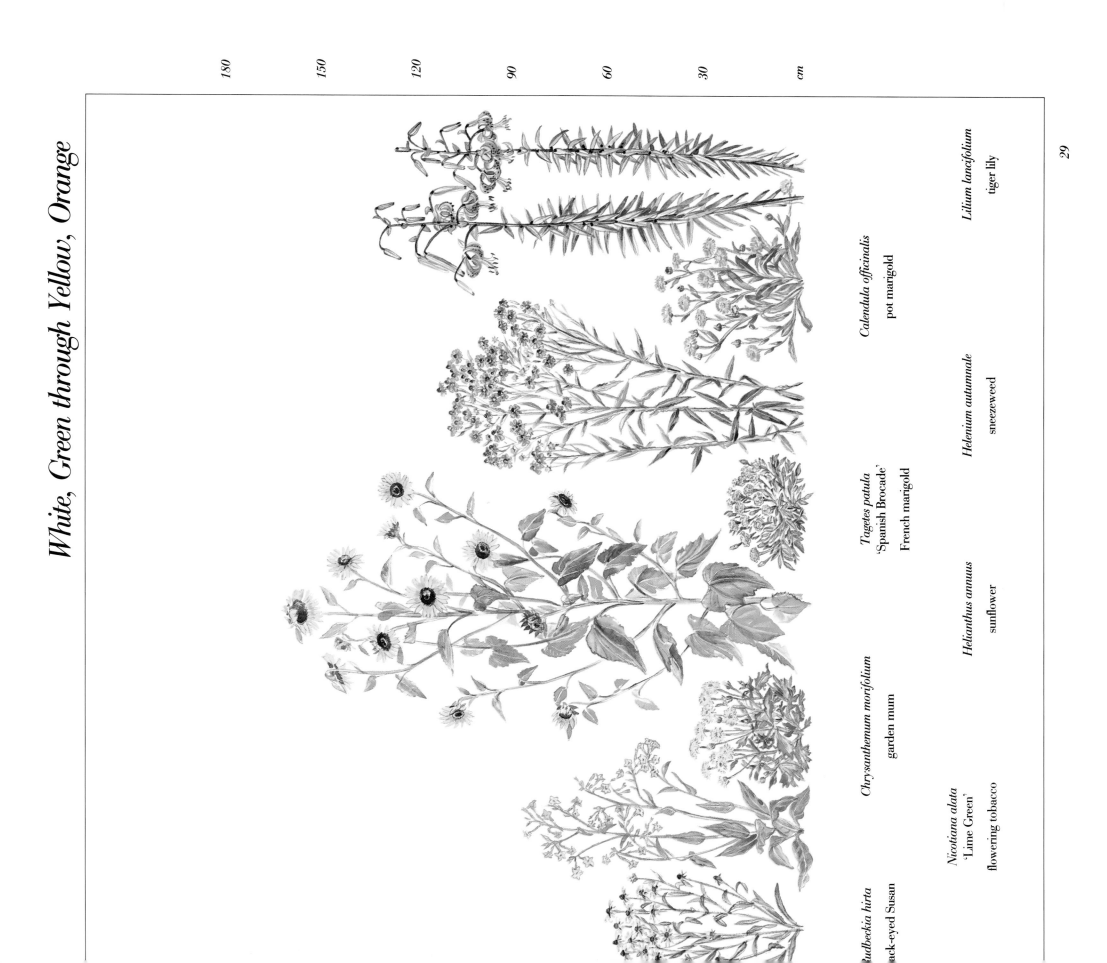

Rudbeckia hirta
black-eyed Susan

Chrysanthemum morifolium
garden mum

Tagetes patula
'Spanish Brocade'
French marigold

Calendula officinalis
pot marigold

Nicotiana alata
'Lime Green'
flowering tobacco

Helianthus annuus
sunflower

Helenium autumnale
sneezeweed

Lilium lancifolium
tiger lily

180

150

120

90

60

30

cm

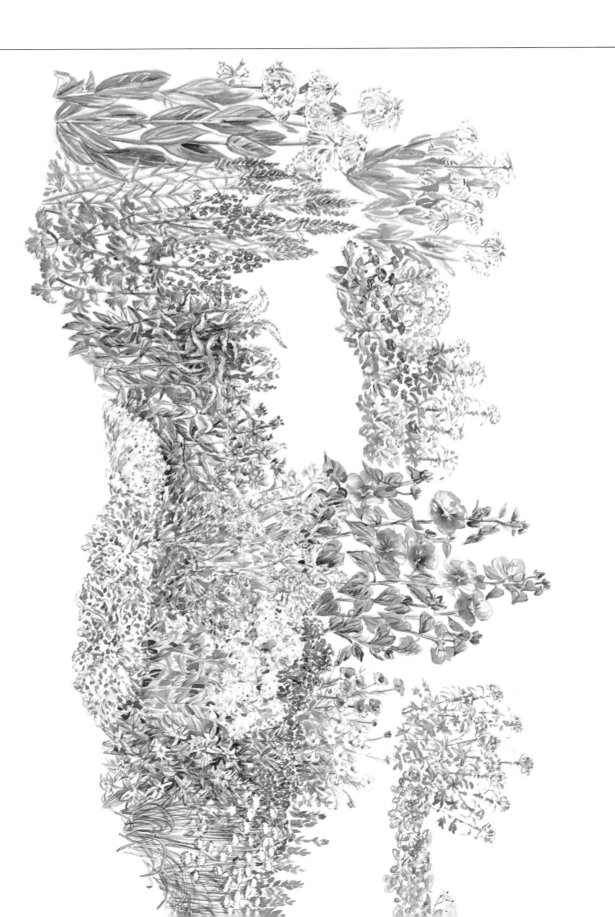

Fall is rich with colors that are warm and ripe, burnished and bold. It also presents a palette so vivid and robust that it can be frivolous and foolish, even shocking and garish. The challenge for us comes in the desire to create a tapestry of harmonious and happy color combinations from a smaller variety of different and hardier plants than is available in either spring or summer.

For the core of the fall garden, we press into ser-vice the best of the daisies, and recognizing that they require companions that are visually different in flower form, growth habit and height, we search for outstanding profile plants and for plants of low or medium height with lush foliage.

In the distance on the left, a border of red zinnias and yellow garden mums, backed by phlox and white cleome and, in the centre, pink cleome, sedum, yellow rudbeckia and, farther to the right, pink daisy chrysanthemums outlines the back edge of an oval courtyard garden. In the foreground and visible from inside and outside the garden are two peninsula borders that flank the entranceway. As we did in spring, we use shades of purple, washes of white and near-white and splashes of yellow to unite the profusion of pink and blue on the left with the blaze of orange on the right.

And in the same way that we had particular

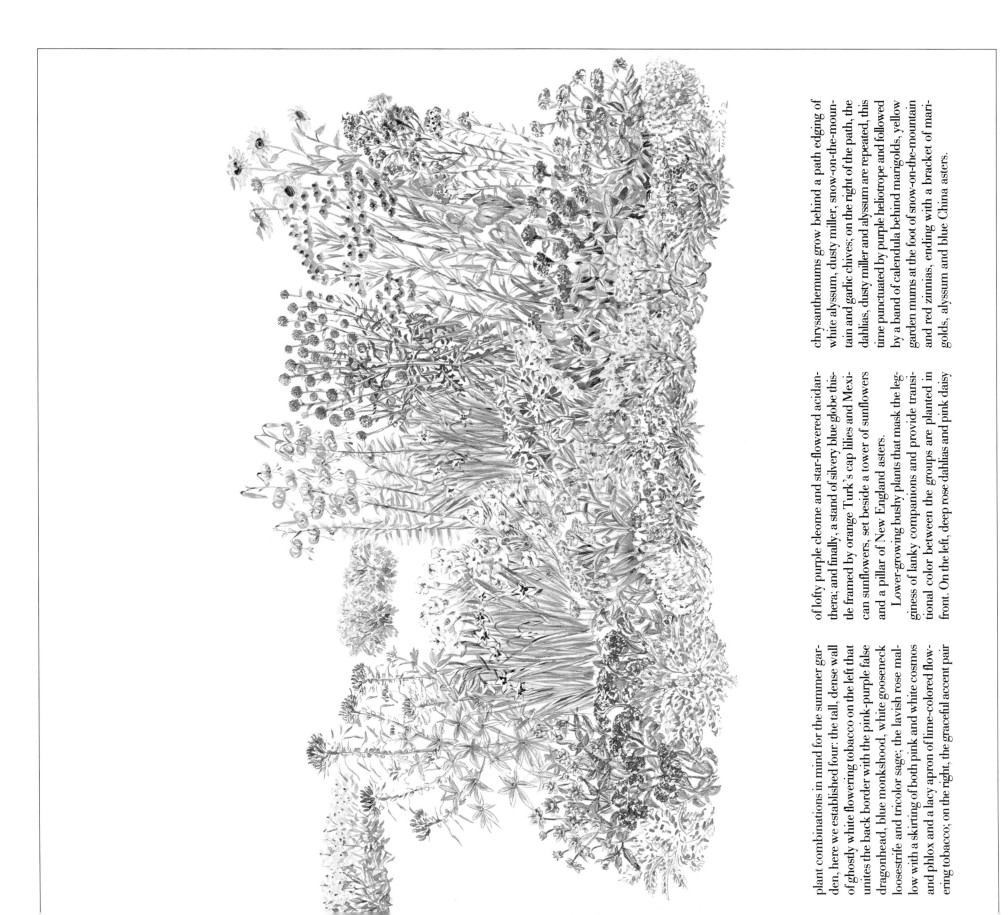

plant combinations in mind for the summer garden, here we established four: the tall, dense wall of ghostly white flowering tobacco on the left that unites the back border with the pink-purple false dragonhead, blue monkshood, white gooseneck loosestrife and tricolor sage; the lavish rose mallow with a skirting of both pink and white cosmos and phlox and a lacy apron of lime-colored flowering tobacco; on the right, the graceful accent pair of lofty purple cleome and star-flowered acidanthera; and finally, a stand of silvery blue globe thistle framed by orange Turk's cap lilies and Mexican sunflowers, set beside a tower of sunflowers and a pillar of New England asters.

Lower-growing bushy plants that mask the legginess of lanky companions and provide transitional color between the groups are planted in front. On the left, deep rose dahlias and pink daisy chrysanthemums grow behind a path edging of white alyssum, dusty miller, snow-on-the-mountain and garlic chives; on the right of the path, the dahlias, dusty miller and alyssum are repeated, this time punctuated by purple heliotrope and followed by a band of calendula behind marigolds, yellow garden mums at the foot of snow-on-the-mountain and red zinnias, ending with a bracket of marigolds, alyssum and blue China asters.

Plant List

Botanical Name	Common Name	Color	Other Colors Available	Light*	Type	Hardiness*	Season
Achillea 'Moonshine'	yarrow	yellow	pink/red/white	sun	perennial	vh	summer
Acidanthera bicolor	acidanthera	white		sun/pt sh	bulb	t	fall
Aconitum napellus 'Bressingham Spire'	monkshood	blue	purple/white	pt sh/sh	perennial	vh	fall
Alcea rosea	hollyhock	pink	red/white/yellow	sun	biennial	h	summer
Alchemilla mollis	lady's mantle	yellow		sun/pt sh	perennial	vh	summer
Allium caeruleum	blue globe onion	blue		sun	bulb	vh	spring
Allium giganteum	giant onion	purple		sun/pt sh	bulb	h	summer
Allium sphaerocephalum	drumstick onion	pink		sun	bulb	vh	summer
Allium tuberosum	garlic chive	white	pink	sun	perennial	vh	summer
Anchusa azurea	Italian bugloss	blue		sun/pt sh	perennial	vh	summer
Anemone blanda 'White Splendour'	windflower	white	blue/pink/purple	sun/pt sh	bulb	mh	spring
Anemone pulsatilla	pasqueflower	purple	blue/red	pt sh	perennial	vh	spring
Anthemis tinctoria	golden marguerite	yellow		sun	perennial	h	summer
Antirrhinum majus 'Rockets'	snapdragon	white	orange/pink/purple/red/yellow	sun	annual	vh	summer
Aquilegia atrata	columbine	purple	pink/red/white/yellow	sun/pt sh	perennial	vh	spring
Aquilegia canadensis	wild columbine	red		sun/pt sh	perennial	vh	spring
Arabis caucasica	wall rock cress	white	purple/white	sun/pt sh	perennial	vh	spring
Armeria maritima	thrift	pink		sun	perennial	vh	spring
Artemisia ludoviciana 'Silver King'	artemisia	green		sun/pt sh	perennial	vh	summer
Artemisia schmidtiana 'Silver Mound'	artemisia	green		sun/pt sh	perennial	vh	summer
Aster novae-angliae	New England aster	purple	pink/white	sun	perennial	vh	fall
Astilbe arendsii	astilbe	red	pink/white	sun/pt sh	perennial	vh	spring
Aubrieta deltoidea	false rock cress	purple		sun/pt sh	perennial	h	spring
Aurinia saxatilis	basket-of-gold	yellow		sun	perennial	vh	spring
Begonia tuberhybrida	tuberous begonia	white	orange/pink/red/yellow	sh	bulb	t	summer
Bergenia cordifolia	heart-leafed bergenia	pink		pt sh	perennial	vh	spring
Calendula officinalis	pot marigold	orange	yellow	sun	annual	mh	summer
Callistephus chinensis	China aster	blue	pink/purple/red/white	sun	annual	vh	fall
Camassia cusickii	camassia	blue		sun	bulb	h	spring
Campanula carpatica	Carpathian harebell	purple	white	sun/pt sh	perennial	vh	summer
Campanula persicifolia	peach-leafed bellflower	white	blue	sun/pt sh	perennial	vh	summer
Centaurea montana	mountain bluet	blue	pink	sun/pt sh	perennial	h	spring
Cerastium tomentosum	snow-in-summer	white		sun	perennial	vh	spring
Chrysanthemum coccineum	painted daisy	pink	red	sun	perennial	vh	summer
Chrysanthemum morifolium	garden mum	yellow	orange/pink/red/white	sun	perennial	vh	fall
Chrysanthemum multicaule 'Gold Plate'	annual chrysanthemum	yellow		sun	annual	mh	summer
Chrysanthemum superbum	shasta daisy	white		sun	perennial	vh	summer
Chrysanthemum zawadskii 'Clara Curtis'	daisy chrysanthemum	pink		sun/pt sh	perennial	vh	fall
Cleome hasslerana	spider flower	purple	pink/white	sun	annual	vh	summer
Convallaria majalis	lily-of-the-valley	white		pt sh/sh	perennial	vh	spring
Coreopsis verticillata 'Moonbeam'	threadleaf coreopsis	yellow		sun	perennial	h	summer
Corydalis lutea	yellow fumitory	yellow		pt sh	perennial	h	summer
Cosmos bipinnatus	cosmos	pink/white	red	sun/pt sh	annual	mh	fall
Crocus flavus	crocus	yellow	orange	sun	bulb	t	spring
Crocus vernus	Dutch crocus	purple	white	sun	bulb	h	spring
Dahlia hybrida	single-flowered dahlia	red	orange/pink/purple/white/yellow	sun	bulb	t	fall
Delphinium grandiflorum 'Blue Elf'	Chinese delphinium	blue	white	sun	perennial	mh	summer
Delphinium 'Pacific Giant'	delphinium	blue	pink/purple/red/white/yellow	sun	perennial	vh	summer
Dianthus deltoides	maiden pink	pink	red	sun	perennial	h	summer
Dianthus superbus 'Super Fantasy'	pink	white	pink/purple/red	sun	perennial	vh	summer
Dicentra eximia	fringed bleeding heart	pink		pt sh/sh	perennial	vh	spring
Dicentra spectabilis	common bleeding heart	pink	white	pt sh/sh	perennial	vh	spring
Dictamnus albus	gas plant	white	pink	sun/pt sh	perennial	vh	spring

Botanical Name	Common Name	Color	Other Colors Available	Light*	Type	Hardiness*	Season
Doronicum cordatum	leopard's bane	yellow		sun/pt sh	perennial	vh	spring
Echinacea purpurea	purple coneflower	pink	white	sun/pt sh	perennial	vh	summer
Echinops ritro	globe thistle	blue		sun/pt sh	perennial	vh	fall
Eranthis hyemalis	winter aconite	yellow		sun/pt sh	bulb	h	spring
Eremurus robustus	foxtail lily	white	orange/pink/yellow	sun	bulb	t	spring
Erigeron speciosus	fleabane	purple	pink	sun/pt sh	perennial	vh	summer
Eschscholzia californica	California poppy	orange	pink/white/yellow	sun	annual		summer
Euphorbia epithymoides	cushion spurge	yellow		sun	perennial	h	spring
Euphorbia marginata	snow-on-the-mountain	green		sun	annual		fall
Fritillaria imperialis	crown imperial	orange	red/yellow	pt sh	bulb	mh	spring
Fritillaria meleagris	checkered lily	pink	purple/white	sun/pt sh	bulb	h	spring
Gaillardia grandiflora	blanketflower	orange	red/yellow	sun	perennial	vh	summer
Galanthus nivalis	common snowdrop	white		pt sh	bulb	vh	spring
Geranium 'Johnson's Blue'	cranesbill	blue	pink	sun/pt sh	perennial	h	spring
Geranium sanguineum	blood-red cranesbill	red	pink	sun/pt sh	perennial	vh	spring
Geum quellyon 'Mrs. Bradshaw'	Chilean avens	red	orange/yellow	sun/pt sh	perennial	h	spring
Gypsophila paniculata	baby's breath	white	pink	sun	perennial	vh	summer
Helenium autumnale	sneezeweed	orange	red/yellow	sun	perennial	vh	fall
Helianthus annuus	sunflower	yellow	orange/red/white	sun	annual		fall
Heliopsis helianthoides	false sunflower	yellow		sun/pt sh	perennial	vh	summer
Heliotropium arborescens 'Lemoine Strain'	heliotrope	purple	blue	sun/pt sh	annual		fall
Helleborus niger	Christmas rose	white		sun/pt sh	perennial	vh	spring
Hemerocallis flava	lemon lily	yellow		sun/pt sh	perennial	vh	spring
Hemerocallis fulva	day lily	orange	pink/red/yellow	sun/pt sh	perennial	vh	summer
Hesperis matronalis	dame's rocket	white	purple	sun/pt sh	perennial	h	spring
Heuchera sanguinea	coral bells	red	pink/white	sun/pt sh	perennial	vh	summer
Hibiscus moscheutos 'Southernbelle'	rose mallow	pink	red/white	sun	perennial	h	fall
Hosta undulata	plantain lily	green		sun/sh	perennial	vh	summer
Hyacinthus orientalis	garden hyacinth	pink	blue/purple/white	sun	bulb	h	spring
Iberis amara	giant hyacinth candytuft	white		sun/pt sh	annual		summer
Iberis sempervirens	evergreen candytuft	white		sun/pt sh	perennial	h	spring
Impatiens walleriana	patience plant	pink	orange/purple/red/white	pt sh/sh	annual		summer
Iris danfordiae	bulbous iris	yellow		sun	bulb	mh	spring
Iris hybrida	bearded iris	pink	white/yellow	sun	perennial	vh	spring
Iris sibirica	Siberian iris	purple	blue/white	sun	perennial	vh	spring
Ixiolirion tataricum	tartar lily	blue		sun	bulb	vh	spring
Lamium maculatum 'White Nancy'	spotted dead nettle	white	purple	sun/sh	perennial	vh	summer
Lavandula angustifolia	English lavender	purple		sun	perennial	mh	summer
Lavatera trimestris	lavatera	pink	white	sun	annual		summer
Liatris spicata	gayfeather	purple	white	sun/pt sh	perennial	vh	summer
Lilium 'Fire King'	Asiatic hybrid lily	orange	pink/red/white/yellow	sun/pt sh	bulb	vh	summer
Lilium lancifolium	tiger lily	orange		sun/pt sh	bulb	h	fall
Lilium 'Pink Perfection'	aurelian hybrid lily	pink	white/yellow	sun/pt sh	bulb	h	summer
Lilium regale	regal lily	white		sun/pt sh	bulb	vh	summer
Linum flavum	golden flax	yellow		sun	perennial	vh	summer
Linum perenne	perennial flax	blue	white	sun	perennial	vh	summer
Lobelia cardinalis	cardinal flower	red		sun/pt sh	perennial	vh	fall
Lobelia erinus	edging lobelia	blue	pink/purple/white	sun/pt sh	annual	vh	summer
Lobularia maritima	sweet alyssum	white	pink/purple	sun/pt sh	annual		summer
Lupinus 'Russell Hybrid'	lupin	red	blue/pink/purple/white/yellow	sun/pt sh	perennial	h	spring
Lychnis arkwrightii 'Salmonaea'	lychnis	orange	red	sun/pt sh	perennial	h	summer
Lychnis chalcedonica	Maltese cross	red	white	sun/pt sh	perennial	vh	summer
Lysimachia clethroides	gooseneck loosestrife	white		sun/pt sh	perennial	vh	fall

Plant List

Botanical Name	Common Name	Color	Other Colors Available	Light*	Type	Hardiness*	Season
Lysimachia punctata	yellow loosestrife	yellow		sun/pt sh	perennial	h	spring
Malva moschata	musk mallow	pink	white	sun/pt sh	perennial	vh	summer
Mertensia virginica	Virginia bluebell	blue		pt sh	perennial	vh	spring
Monarda didyma	bee balm	red	pink/white	sun/pt sh	perennial	vh	summer
Muscari armeniacum	grape hyacinth	blue		sun	bulb	vh	spring
Myosotis sylvatica	forget-me-not	blue	purple/white	sun	perennial	h	spring
Narcissus poeticus 'Actea'	poet's narcissus	white	pink/white	pt sh	bulb	h	spring
Narcissus 'Suzy'	jonquil narcissus	orange		sun	bulb	h	spring
Narcissus 'White Plume'	daffodil	white	yellow	sun/pt sh	bulb	h	spring
Nicotiana alata 'Lime Green'	flowering tobacco	green		sun/pt sh	annual		fall
Nicotiana sylvestris	flowering tobacco	white	pink/red/white	sun/pt sh	annual		fall
Nolana paradoxa 'Bluebird'	nolana	blue		sun	annual		summer
Oenothera tetragona	sundrop	yellow	red	sun	perennial	h	summer
Paeonia officinalis	peony	pink/white	red/white	sun/pt sh	perennial	vh	spring
Papaver orientale	Oriental poppy	orange/pink		sun	perennial	vh	spring
Papaver rhoeas	Flanders poppy	red	orange/pink/white	sun	annual		summer
Pelargonium hortorum	geranium	red	orange/pink/white	sun	annual		summer
Petunia hybrida	petunia	purple	blue/pink/red/white/yellow	sun/pt sh	annual		fall
Phlox paniculata	garden phlox	red/white	pink/purple	sun/pt sh	perennial	vh	summer
Phlox subulata	moss pink	pink	blue/white	sun	perennial	vh	spring
Physostegia virginiana	false dragonhead	purple	white	sun/pt sh	perennial	vh	fall
Platycodon grandiflorus	balloon flower	purple	pink/white	sun/pt sh	perennial	vh	summer
Polygonatum odoratum	Solomon's seal	white		pt sh/sh	perennial	vh	spring
Primula sieboldii	Japanese star primrose	pink	purple/white	pt sh	perennial	h	spring
Primula veris	cowslip primrose	yellow		pt sh	perennial	h	spring
Puschkinia scilloides	striped squill	white		pt sh	perennial	h	spring
Rudbeckia hirta	black-eyed Susan	yellow		sun/pt sh	perennial	vh	fall
Salvia splendens 'Empire Red'	scarlet sage	red	pink/purple/white	sun/pt sh	annual		summer
Salvia viridis	tricolor sage	purple	blue/pink/white	sun/pt sh	annual		fall
Scabiosa caucasica	pincushion flower	blue	pink/white	sun	perennial	vh	summer
Scilla sibirica	Siberian squill	blue	white	sun/sh	bulb	vh	spring
Sedum spectabile	showy stonecrop	pink	red/white	sun/pt sh	perennial	vh	fall
Senecio cineraria	dusty miller	green		sun	annual		fall
Stachys grandiflora	big betony	purple		sun/pt sh	perennial	vh	summer
Tagetes patula 'Spanish Brocade'	French marigold	orange	yellow	sun	annual		fall
Thalictrum aquilegifolium	columbine meadow rue	pink	purple/white	sun/pt sh	perennial	vh	spring
Tithonia rotundifolia	Mexican sunflower	orange	yellow	sun	annual		summer
Tradescantia andersoniana	spiderwort	white	pink/purple	sun/pt sh	perennial	vh	summer
Tropaeolum majus 'Whirlybird'	bedding nasturtium	orange	red/yellow	sun	annual		summer
Tulipa clusiana chrysantha	candy-stick tulip	orange		sun	bulb	h	spring
Tulipa 'Diana'	single-flowered tulip	white	pink/purple/red/yellow	sun	bulb	vh	spring
Tulipa fosterana 'Orange Emperor'	fosterana tulip	orange	pink/white/yellow	sun	bulb	vh	spring
Tulipa 'Red Shine'	lily-flowered tulip	red	pink/white/yellow	sun	bulb	vh	spring
Valeriana officinalis	valerian	white	pink	sun/sh	perennial	vh	summer
Veronica latifolia	Hungarian speedwell	blue		sun	perennial	vh	summer
Viola tricolor	Johnny-jump-up	purple		pt sh	perennial	vh	summer
Viola wittrockiana 'Spring Magic Moonlight'	pansy	yellow	blue/orange/pink/purple/white	sun/pt sh	annual		summer
Yucca filamentosa	Adam's needle	white		sun	perennial	mh	summer
Zinnia elegans 'Pulcino'	zinnia	red	orange/pink/white/yellow	sun	annual		fall

Key to Abbreviations

Light Needs: sh = shade; pt = part. Hardiness refers to the cold tolerance of biennials, perennials and bulbs: vh = very hardy; h = hardy; mh = moderately hardy (needs adequate snow cover or other protection); t = tender (lift and store indoors over the winter).

The American Horticultural Society Flower Finder, by Jacqueline Hériteau & André Viette. Simon and Schuster, New York, 1992.

Annuals, by James Underwood Crockett. The Time-Life Encyclopedia of Gardening, Time-Life Books, New York, 1972.

Annuals: Yearly Classics for the Contemporary Garden, by Rob Proctor. HarperCollins, New York, 1991.

The Art of Planting, by Graham Stuart Thomas. J.M. Dent & Sons in association with The National Trust, London, 1984.

The Art of Planting, by Rosemary Verey. Little, Brown, Boston, 1990.

Beds and Borders: Traditional and Original Garden Designs, by Wendy B. Murphy. Houghton Mifflin, Boston, 1990.

Bulbs, by James Underwood Crockett. The Time-Life Encyclopedia of Gardening, Time-Life Books, New York, 1972.

The Canadian Gardener: A Guide to Gardening in Canada, by Marjorie Harris. Random House, Toronto, 1990.

Color in My Garden, by Louise Beebe Wilder. The Atlantic Monthly Press, New York, 1990.

Designing a Garden: A Guide to Planning and Planting Through the Seasons, by Allen Paterson. Camden House, Camden East, Ontario, 1992.

Garden Style, by Penelope Hobhouse. Little, Brown, Boston, 1988.

The Harrowsmith Annual Garden, by Jennifer Bennett & Turid Forsyth. Camden House, Camden East, Ontario, 1990.

The Harrowsmith Perennial Garden, by Patrick Lima. Camden House, Camden East, Ontario, 1987.

The Illustrated Gertrude Jekyll: Colour Schemes for the Flower Garden, by Gertrude Jekyll. Little, Brown, Boston, 1988.

In a Canadian Garden, by Nicole Eaton & Hilary Weston. Penguin Books, Markham, Ontario, 1989.

Monet's Passion: Ideas, Inspiration and Insights From the Painter's Gardens, by Elizabeth Murray. Pomegranate Artbooks, San Francisco, 1989.

The Natural Garden, by Ken Druse. Clarkson N. Potter, New York, 1989.

Perennials, by James Underwood Crockett. The Time-Life Encyclopedia of Gardening, Time-Life Books, New York, 1972.

Perennials: How to Select, Grow and Enjoy, by Pamela Harper & Frederick McGourty. HP Books, Tucson, Arizona, 1985.

Perennials for the Prairies, by Edgar W. Toop & Sara Williams. University of Alberta, Edmonton, 1991.

Spring Flowers: A Harrowsmith Gardener's Guide, edited by Katharine Ferguson. Camden House, Camden East, Ontario, 1989.

Taylor's Guide to Annuals, Taylor's Guide to Bulbs, Taylor's Guide to Perennials. Chanticleer Press, New York. Based on Taylor's Encyclopedia of Gardening, Houghton Mifflin, Boston, 1961.